Animal Parts

Animal Mouths

By Connor Stratton

level
2
little blue
readers

www.littlebluehousebooks.com

Little Blue House is distributed by North Star Editions:
sales@northstareditions.com | 888-417-0195

Produced for Little Blue House by Red Line Editorial.

Photographs ©: iStockphoto, cover, 4, 7, 11 (top), 11 (bottom), 12, 14–15, 16–17, 18, 21 (top), 21 (bottom), 22–23, 24 (top left), 24 (top right), 24 (bottom left), 24 (bottom right); Shutterstock Images, 8–9

Library of Congress Control Number: 2020900864

ISBN
978-1-64619-178-9 (hardcover)
978-1-64619-212-0 (paperback)
978-1-64619-280-9 (ebook pdf)
978-1-64619-246-5 (hosted ebook)

Printed in the United States of America
Mankato, MN
082020

About the Author

Connor Stratton enjoys spotting new animals and writing books for children. He lives in Minnesota.

Table of Contents

Animal Mouths

Animals have mouths.

Animal mouths

are different.

Lions have mouths.

Lions live on land.

Sharks have mouths.

Sharks live in the water.

Birds have mouths.
Birds can fly through
the air.

Teeth

Some animals have teeth in their mouths.

Elephants have huge teeth. These teeth are called tusks.

Some animals have
no teeth.

Turtles have no teeth.

turtle

Tongues

Many animals

have tongues.

Tongues help animals eat.

Some tongues are long.
Lizards can have
long tongues.
Anteaters have long
tongues too.

Some tongues are split.

Snakes have split tongues.

split tongue

snake

Glossary

elephant

snake

lion

turtle

Index